UNSUNG HEROES OF
US HISTORY

by Todd Kortemeier

12 STORY LIBRARY

www.12StoryLibrary.com

12-Story Library is an imprint of Peterson Publishing Company and Press Room Editions.

Produced for 12-Story Library by Red Line Editorial

Photographs ©: Bettmann/Corbis, cover, 1, 16, 27; Corbis, 4, 22; North Wind Picture Archives, 5, 13, 23; Thomas J. O'Halloran/US News & World Report Magazine Photograph Collection/Library of Congress, 6; Library of Congress, 7, 14; Percy Moran/Library of Congress, 8; damaloney/iStockphoto, 9; Ruth Fremson/AP Images, 11; Louis S. Glanzman/National Geographic/Getty Images, 12; Harris & Ewing Collection/Library of Congress, 15, 29; M. Spencer Green/AP Images, 17; George Grantham Bain Collection/Library of Congress, 18, 19, 28; Jeannie Nuss/AP Images, 21; Detroit Publishing Co./Library of Congress, 25; Frank Leslie's Illustrated Newspaper/Library of Congress, 26

Library of Congress Cataloging-in-Publication Data
Names: Kortemeier, Todd, 1986- author.
Title: Unsung heroes of U.S. history / by Todd Kortemeier.
Other titles: Unsung heroes of United States history
Description: North Mankato, MN : 12-Story Library, Peterson Publishing
    Company, 2017. | Series: Unsung heroes | Includes bibliographical
    references and index.
Identifiers: LCCN 2016002374 (print) | LCCN 2016006612 (ebook) | ISBN
    9781632353122 (library bound : alk. paper) | ISBN 9781632353627 (pbk. :
    alk. paper) | ISBN 9781621434764 (hosted ebook)
Subjects: LCSH: Heroes--United States--Biography--Juvenile literature. |
    United States--Biography--Juvenile literature.
Classification: LCC CT217 .K67 2016 (print) | LCC CT217 (ebook) | DDC
    920.073--dc23
LC record available at http://lccn.loc.gov/2016002374

Printed in the United States of America
Mankato, MN
May, 2016

Access free, up-to-date content on this topic plus a full digital version of this book. Scan the QR code on page 31 or use your school's login at 12StoryLibrary.com.

Table of Contents

James Armistead Helps at the Battle of Yorktown

Many black soldiers fought in the American Revolution. Some of them were free, and some were enslaved. Both the American and British sides also used slaves as spies. James Armistead was one of these spies. The British thought he was working for them. But Armistead was really working for the Americans. He gave the British all the wrong information.

Armistead was born into slavery in 1760. When the revolution came, he joined the American side. He had to get his owner's permission to serve. He was assigned to the Marquis de Lafayette. Lafayette was a French military officer on the American side of the war. Lafayette first used Armistead as a messenger.

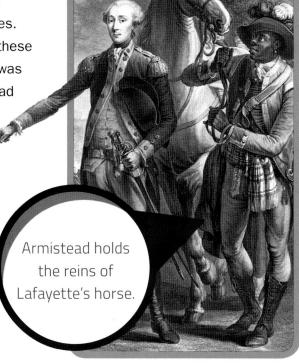

Armistead holds the reins of Lafayette's horse.

But he soon saw Armistead's ability to be a convincing spy.

Armistead posed as a runaway slave. He knew the Virginia

$40

Amount that Armistead was awarded per year for his services during the war.

- Armistead was a slave who served the American side of the American Revolution.
- Posing as a runaway slave, he gathered important strategy from the British side.
- The information Armistead gathered was used to win the Battle of Yorktown.

countryside well. The British needed guidance there. The British officers suspected nothing and freely discussed strategy in front of Armistead. Armistead reported all of this back to Lafayette.

In July 1781, Armistead learned that 10,000 British troops were heading to Yorktown, Virginia. Lafayette told George Washington. Washington concentrated his forces on the town. The Americans were able to halt the British forces and win the Battle of Yorktown. By October, the British surrendered.

Armistead's help was critical in winning this important battle. Despite his role in helping the American troops, he was not freed from slavery until 1787. Armistead was grateful to Lafayette and added that name onto his. He went by James Armistead Lafayette for the rest of his life. He farmed in Virginia until he passed away at the age of 72.

Armistead helped American forces win the Battle of Yorktown.

Shirley Chisholm Gets Elected to Congress

The Voting Rights Act of 1965 forever changed the politics of the United States. The act made it illegal to prevent people from voting because of their race. Black people could now fully participate in democracy. Shirley Chisholm would help give them a voice.

In 1964, Chisholm won a seat in the New York State Senate. She stood up for what she believed in. She tried to make people's lives better. For this she was known as "Fighting Shirley." Then, in 1968, she jumped into national politics. She ran for a seat in the US House of Representatives. She had already been an activist in her neighborhood. Now, she promised to keep representing those interests on the national stage.

Chisholm won the election. She became the first black woman ever elected to Congress. Chisholm wanted to bring attention to her causes. She believed people should get help from the government to pay for education. She thought parents should have easier access to child care.

In 1969, she used her first speech to Congress to denounce the Vietnam War.

Chisholm wanted to help people.

6

Like many Americans, she didn't think the United States should be involved in the war. She also served on several committees, including the Rules Committee. This important committee determines how bills are debated in the House. It previously had only one female member.

But Chisholm had bigger ideas. She decided to run for president in 1972. She was the first black woman ever to do so. Chisholm got her name on the primary ballot in 12 states. At the party convention, she received 152 votes, about 10 percent of the total. It wasn't much, but it represented huge progress.

Chisholm was the first black woman to run for president.

BRING U.S. TOGETHER

VOTE **CHISHOLM** 1972
UNBOUGHT AND UNBOSSED

Chisholm retired from Congress in 1983. When asked why she ran for president, the reason was simple. Somebody had to do it first.

CHISHOLM'S LATER LIFE

In 1993, President Bill Clinton nominated Chisholm to serve as the US ambassador to Jamaica. Because of poor health, she was unable to accept. Chisholm had Caribbean roots, having lived in Barbados when she was young. She passed away in 2005.

7
Number of terms Chisholm served in the US House of Representatives.

- Chisholm was first elected to the New York State Senate in 1964.
- She was the first black woman elected to the US Congress.
- Chisholm ran for president in 1972.

Polly Cooper Saves American Troops

The American Revolution was not fought only by the military. Many different people from all walks of life helped make America free. The Oneida people were one of six Iroquois Nations. They were the only ones to support the American Revolution. Oneidas served as soldiers and spies fighting for American independence from Great Britain.

When fall turned to winter in 1777, US General George Washington's troops were in bad shape. The winter at Valley Forge, Pennsylvania, was bitterly cold. The soldiers were hungry and freezing. Oneida Chief Shenandoah sent a group of his people with supplies to help the army. Polly Cooper was one of them.

Cooper and the other Oneidas brought the Americans white corn. The Oneidas were familiar with white corn. But it was quite different from the yellow kind that the colonial soldiers were used to. The starving troops tried to eat the corn without cooking it. But Cooper knew that

Washington and his troops at Valley Forge

would make them deathly sick. She showed the soldiers how to cook and prepare the corn.

After the other Oneidas returned home, Cooper stayed behind to help. She taught Washington's men about

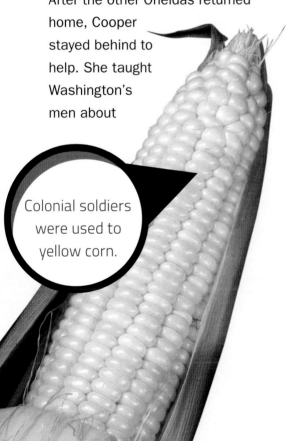

Colonial soldiers were used to yellow corn.

nutrition. She showed them what foods were good to eat. She even became the cook for George Washington and his wife, Martha, at Valley Forge.

Cooper did not accept any money her help. Instead, Martha Washington gave Cooper a black scarf as a gift. It is still treasured by the Oneida people. Cooper was not finished helping though. She cooked for US troops during the War of 1812 too.

John R. Fox Sacrifices Himself for His Country

Many black people proudly served their country during World War II. By the war's end, 1.2 million black people were in service around the world. But the military was segregated until 1948, after the war. At first, black people could have only noncombat roles on the home front. But as the war continued, more and more soldiers were needed at the front lines.

One of these brave soldiers was John R. Fox. He was an army first lieutenant serving in Italy. On December 26, 1944, his unit was holding its position. The town that they were in was slowly being overtaken by enemy Germans. Fox and his fellow soldiers did what they could. But many of them were forced to retreat. There was no question that the enemy would soon control the town.

Fox waited, ordering more attacks on the advancing Germans. But as the Germans got closer, so did the gunfire. It got very close to Fox's position. He ordered one more attack, knowing it would be right on top of him. He knew the attack

4

Hours that Fox was able to hold off the German forces before the last attack.

- Fox was an American soldier serving in Italy.
- The enemy German army was advancing on his position. Fox held them off with artillery attacks.
- Fox ordered the last attack knowing that it would be close enough to him to kill him.
- The Medal of Honor was awarded to Fox 53 years after his death.

would kill him, but it would save the town. Fox's final artillery attack pressed the Germans back.

Americans were able to retake the town. When they did, they found Fox's body lying among hundreds of fallen German soldiers. He had sacrificed himself for his country. Normally, such a heroic action would earn the Medal of Honor. It is the highest honor in the military. But black people were not eligible for this award at this time.

In 1993, the US Army launched a research project. The goal was to identify soldiers who should have earned medals. Fox was one of seven black soldiers to earn the Medal of Honor in 1997.

Fox's widow Arlene Fox held his Medal of Honor after it was posthumously awarded in 1997.

5

Sybil Ludington Makes Her Own Midnight Ride

Enemy British forces were approaching. A patriot rode out into the night to warn the Americans. This might sound like the tale of Paul Revere. But it's the story of Sybil Ludington, who rode twice as far as Revere.

Sybil Ludington's father was Henry Ludington. He was a colonel in the colonial army. On April 26, 1777, there was a knock at the door. It was a messenger with news. He said 2,000 British troops were attacking nearby Danbury in western Connecticut. Colonel Ludington needed to act. But his troops were scattered. They didn't expect this to happen.

Colonel Ludington's 16-year-old daughter, Sybil, jumped on her

A portrait of Sybil Ludington's ride

Sybil Ludington

400

Number of American soldiers that Sybil rounded up during her ride.

- Sybil was 16 years old at the time of her ride.
- Her father was a colonel in the colonial army.
- British troops were advancing on Sybil's hometown.
- She rode through the night to warn the Americans and gather up soldiers.

horse, named Star. Sybil and Star rode 40 miles (64 km) through the night. She warned anyone who would listen that the British were coming. She told soldiers to meet at her house. Sybil had to avoid British soldiers and anyone who was loyal to the British. On top of that, there was no moon, making the ride dark and dangerous.

Unfortunately, the troops arrived too late to save the town. But they were able to fight the British and push them back. Sybil received a thank you from George Washington for her efforts. But her ride was soon forgotten in favor of Revere's.

SYBIL'S LEGACY

Paul Revere might have poems and songs written about him. But Sybil is remembered in other ways. Since 1979, a footrace has been held in her honor. It retraces the route of her famous ride.

Sybil had to watch out for British soldiers as she rode.

Frances Perkins Helps FDR Pass the New Deal

Frances Perkins had many accomplishments before being named US secretary of labor. She had a degree in political science. She had worked on New York state committees to improve the lives of workers. By any measure, she was a great choice to be secretary of labor. But this was 1933. No woman had ever held a cabinet position before. When President Franklin Delano Roosevelt selected her for the position, the decision was immediately questioned.

Some people believed that only a man should be secretary of labor. They wrote letters to the president. They urged him to pick someone else. But Perkins just went to work. There was a lot to do. The effects of the Great Depression were still being felt. More than 13 million Americans were out of work.

To help lift the country out of the Depression, President Roosevelt proposed a "New Deal" for Americans. This was a series of programs to get people back to work. With Perkins' experience leading workers, she helped with this effort. Perkins worked hard for the New Deal.

Perkins helped get people back to work during the Great Depression.

In 1933, she gave more than 100 speeches to generate support for it.

One of Perkins's biggest contributions to the New Deal was her work on Social Security. This program is still around today. It makes sure people have money to live on when they retire. Perkins was head of the committee that prepared the proposal for Social Security for Congress. Her committee presented the plan to Roosevelt, who presented it to Congress two days later.

The New Deal is usually credited to Roosevelt. But it would not have been the same without Perkins. She promoted a fair minimum wage, 40-hour workweeks, and the end of

12
Number of years Perkins served as secretary of labor, the longest term ever in this position.

- Perkins was the first female cabinet member.
- She had an extensive background in labor relations and politics.
- As secretary, Perkins promoted policies to help workers.
- Many of her policies were part of President Roosevelt's New Deal.

child labor. Almost all of the policies that she wanted to enact made it into the New Deal.

Perkins was one of few women working for the federal government in the mid-1900s.

Casimir Pulaski: Father of the American Cavalry

Casimir Pulaski grew up believing in patriotic causes. At only 22, he fought for a revolution and against an unjust king. But this wasn't in the United States. It was in Pulaski's home country of Poland.

Pulaski's bravery and military skill were noticed beyond Poland. American patriot Benjamin Franklin met Pulaski in France in 1775. Hearing tales of his heroics, he told George Washington. Washington wanted Pulaski on his side. Pulaski came to America. But other American soldiers were not convinced. To them, Pulaski was a foreigner. They didn't believe he was loyal. So Washington assigned Pulaski a unit of mainly foreign troops.

Pulaski's unit became one of the best cavalries on the American side. He taught his unit how to ride up close to British forces, undetected. They observed enemy movements and

Pulaski led his cavalry to victory in the American Revolution.

A man wears a traditional Polish military uniform for Casimir Pulaski Day in Illinois.

Wherever they went, Pulaski's men helped win the war.

The Battle of Savannah was Pulaski's last. He courageously charged into battle on horseback. But a cannon blast struck him. He died days later on October 15, 1779. But Pulaski's leadership and influence lived on. To this day, he is known as the "Father of the American Cavalry."

strategy. If American forces had to retreat, Pulaski's men were there to keep the British away. They ended a British assault of Charleston, South Carolina. They recaptured Savannah, Georgia, from British hands.

CASIMIR PULASKI DAY

Polish-born Pulaski was not as well remembered as other American heroes. But to his fellow Polish Americans, he was a hero. They made sure his contributions to American independence lived on. Casimir Pulaski Day is a public holiday in the state of Illinois. The state is home to a large Polish population.

34
Pulaski's age when he died of a battle wound.

- Pulaski was born in Poland.
- He fought for freedom in his native country.
- His achievements there got him attention from American patriot leaders.
- Pulaski developed many important cavalry techniques.
- He helped the Americans win the American Revolution.

Jeannette Rankin Takes a Stand for Peace

It was amazing enough that Jeannette Rankin was elected to the House of Representatives in 1916. She was the first woman ever elected. Women in the United States did not have the right to vote at that time. But being a woman and an antiwar activist was even more rare. Rankin became known for her antiwar views.

Shortly after Rankin's election, the world changed. World War I broke out in 1914. Rankin didn't believe in war. In 1917, she voted against the United States entering the war. Only 49 others joined her as the House voted 374-50 to go to war. Some people said that if Rankin didn't support the war, she supported the enemy. They called her anti-American.

After her term ended, she remained active in fighting for her causes. She worked with women's rights

People gathered for an antiwar meeting in New York City.

6

Number of women in Congress besides Rankin during her second term.

- Rankin was the first woman elected to the US Congress.
- She was one of 50 people to vote against entering World War I.
- She was the only one to vote against entering World War II.

THINK ABOUT IT

Rankin stood up for what she believed in. But her beliefs were extremely unpopular. Have you ever had an unpopular opinion? How did you handle it?

groups. She advocated for world peace. By the late 1930s, war was again looming. In 1940, Rankin was once again elected to the House of Representatives.

By 1940, World War II was already underway, but the United States was not involved. Rankin worked to keep it that way. She voted against any US involvement in the war. But when Japan bombed Pearl Harbor in Hawaii, there was almost unanimous support for declaring war. Rankin stuck to her beliefs. She was the only member in the entire House to vote against it.

Rankin suffered hisses and boos from the other House members.

She needed police protection to get back to her office. She was unable to do much with the rest of her term. Though unpopular, she never wavered in her beliefs. Even at the time of her death in 1973, she was considering a House run to protest the Vietnam War.

Rankin promoted peace.

Bass Reeves Helps Tame the Wild West

In the late 1800s, the territory now known as Oklahoma was truly wild. It was home to countless criminals. Law and order were rare. In 1875, President Ulysses S. Grant ordered the territory cleaned up. He had 200 US marshals hired. One man in particular was a perfect fit for the job.

Bass Reeves was black and born in the South. So, he was born into slavery. He escaped when he ran away to fight for the Union during the Civil War. In his travels, he learned American Indian languages. He later settled in the Oklahoma territory. Using his knowledge of language and weapons, Reeves was well suited to the dangerous land.

Reeves could not read or write. But he was very intelligent. He gained a reputation for arresting criminals whom other marshals couldn't catch. Reeves sometimes used disguises to get close to criminals. He arrested more than 3,000 of them in his 32-year career. In one case, a criminal turned herself in rather than be hunted by him. Reeves once arrested his own son after his son was charged with murder.

As the South became more populated, things changed. The same people who once supported slavery returned to power.

75,000
Size of the territory, in square miles (120,701 sq. km), that Reeves was charged with patrolling.

- Reeves was born a slave, but escaped.
- He became a US marshal assigned to the lawless Oklahoma territory.
- He was one of the most effective marshals in the history of the Wild West.

A statue of Bass Reeves in Fort Smith, Arkansas

THE LONE RANGER

Most cowboys are depicted in movies and on television as white men. But there were many black cowboys, too, like Reeves. Some believe that Reeves was the inspiration for the television series *The Lone Ranger.*

Black marshals found it difficult to get hired. Reeves retired in 1907. He was a police officer for a short time. He passed away in 1910. His achievements were known to locals, but forgotten elsewhere. It is not even known where he was buried. A US Marshals Museum in Fort Smith, Arkansas, features an exhibit on Reeves, now known as one of the greatest lawmen ever.

Robert Smalls Captures a Southern Ship

Robert Smalls' life was unusual for an enslaved boy born in 1839. His mother worked in the home of a slave owner. Smalls grew up in the house and played with both white and black children. He became resistant to the racist rules that black people were expected to follow.

A portrait of Robert Smalls

Smalls' mother feared that his attitude would get him into trouble. When he was 12, she sent him to work in Charleston, South Carolina. He worked on the docks and learned a lot about ships and sailing. By the age of 22, he'd earned a spot on the crew of a ship.

One night, a year into the Civil War, Smalls' ship, the *Planter*, was at the dock. Its Confederate white crew left for the night. Only the eight-slave crew was left on board. Smalls saw an opportunity. He gave instructions to the crew and took the captain's wheel. The men had to sail through Confederate territory. They kept

$1,500

Reward that Smalls was given for delivering the *Planter* into Union hands.

- Smalls was born into slavery, the son of a housekeeper.
- From an early age, he rebelled against slavery.
- Smalls became a dockworker, then a sailor.
- Using his skills, he took control of a ship and sailed to freedom.

flying the flag. Smalls did nothing out of the ordinary.

When they reached northern waters, they raised a white flag. They wanted to show they were surrendering. The Union soldiers saw that there were no enemies on board. They welcomed the ship into the safety of the North. Smalls had won his freedom. He also was able to give important military knowledge to the Union.

Smalls delivered the *Planter* to the Union.

Elizabeth Van Lew Spies for the Union

The unlikeliest of spies lived in the unlikeliest place. Elizabeth Van Lew was a 43-year-old single woman from Richmond, Virginia. Richmond was the capital of the Confederacy during the Civil War. Richmond's citizens were loyal to the southern side. But Van Lew always considered herself a northerner. She decided she would help the Union. But she pretended to be loyal to the Confederacy.

There were many jobs and duties women were not allowed to perform. So nobody suspected that Van Lew was secretly helping the enemy. She lived very close to a military prison. Many Union soldiers were held there. Van Lew brought them food, medicine, and books. This earned her a lot of scorn from southerners. But they didn't know she was doing

even more. There were messages hidden in secret compartments of the dishes in which she brought food. They contained updates on the war and information to help the prisoners escape.

Van Lew also got information from the prisoners. Because they had been captured, they knew enemy positions. Van Lew got this information to General

12

Approximate number of spies working for Van Lew at the peak of the Civil War.

- Van Lew was a supporter of the Union while she lived in the South.
- She remained loyal to the Union.
- She aided Union prisoners and exchanged information with them.

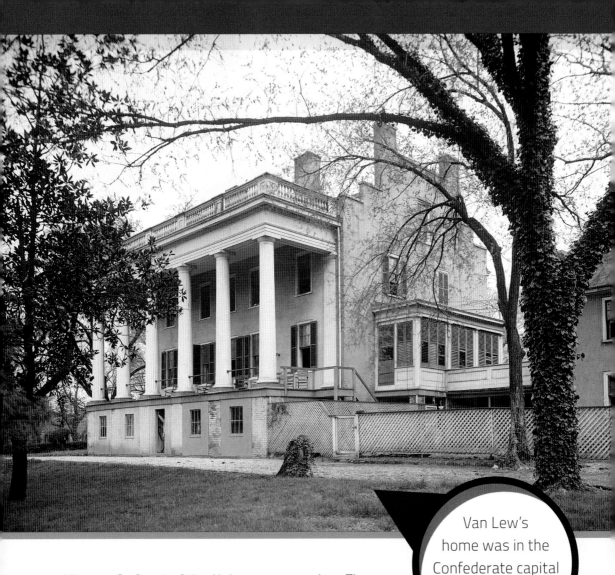

Ulysses S. Grant of the Union army. Van Lew also knew people inside the Confederate government. They provided her with information as well.

After the Union won the war, Van Lew was thanked for her efforts. General Grant got her a job as postmaster of Richmond. But the people of Richmond never forgave her. They also looked down on her views on women's rights. She lived as an outcast in Richmond for the rest of her life. But her work got her inducted into the Military Intelligence Hall of Fame.

Van Lew's home was in the Confederate capital of Richmond, Virginia.

Victoria Woodhull Runs for President

Victoria Woodhull would become known for defying people's expectations of women. But as a young woman, those expectations almost trapped her. She was married at 14. She had a baby a year later. Her husband mistreated her, and she divorced him. Divorce was highly unusual and looked down on. Woodhull's next husband was different. He encouraged her to get an education and work to further the cause of women's rights.

Through her husband's connections Woodhull met Cornelius Vanderbilt. He was a famous builder of railroads. With his help, Woodhull and her sister opened up a financial firm. They were the first women to trade stocks on Wall Street. The sisters also started a newspaper that reported on women's issues. In 1870, Woodhull

Woodhull gave speeches to government officials supporting women's right to vote.

announced something even more radical. She would run for president in the 1872 election.

Woodhull was a member of the Equal Rights Party. Party members believed in equal rights for all genders and races. Women were huge supporters of Woodhull. But at the time, women weren't allowed to vote. Woodhull herself couldn't be president. The Constitution says the president must be 35 years old. Woodhull would have been 34.

Still, Woodhull's campaign caused a stir. Critics looked for any reason to degrade her. Three days before the election, she was put in jail. She was charged with running an "indecent" newspaper. After a trial, she was found not guilty. But her reputation was ruined.

It's unknown exactly how many votes Woodhull received in the election. But by challenging the system, she made more people aware of women's rights.

48

Years between Woodhull's run for president and when women were granted the right to vote.

- Woodhull worked for women's rights.
- In 1872, she was the first female candidate for president.
- She was jailed for indecency because of prejudice.

Woodhull was an advocate for women's rights.

THINK ABOUT IT

Woodhull was the first woman to run for president. It was very unlikely that she would win. Why do you think she ran anyway?

27

Fact Sheet

- Africans had been enslaved in North America long before the United States was founded. The Dutch first brought slaves to Jamestown, Virginia, in 1619. Slaves were a key part of the new country's economy. Slaves also fought on the American side in the American Revolution. After that war, people's attitudes about slavery began to change. The Civil War was fought over this issue, as the Confederate South relied heavily on slaves for its economy. The antislavery North won the war. President Abraham Lincoln signed the Emancipation Proclamation, which outlawed slavery, on January 1, 1863.

- British colonists encountered American Indians soon after arriving in what is now the United States. Some of these relationships were positive. The American Indians showed colonists how to farm and use the land. Colonists gave the natives tools and other modern conveniences. But there also was much conflict. Settlers expanded their territory, taking land from the American Indians.

- From its first writing, the Constitution of the United States established rights for white men. Women, black people, and other minorities had fewer rights. The 14th and 15th Amendments gave voting and citizen rights to freed black slaves. But women were still without such rights. By the mid-1800s, groups emerged to argue for women's rights. But it wasn't until 1920 that the 19th Amendment passed, giving women the right to vote. However, issues of gender discrimination continue to this day.

- Black people had voting rights since the 1800s. But there were laws in the United States that segregated them from many aspects of society. Black people weren't allowed to go certain places. Schools were either for black people or for white people. In the 1950s and 1960s, these laws were routinely challenged. People engaged in protests to try to force change. The Civil Rights Act of 1964 made segregation and race discrimination illegal. Despite the new laws, black people and other minorities still face racism.

Glossary

ambassador
A person who represents his or her country in official relations with another country.

artillery
Military weapons that fire missiles.

cabinet
A group of advisers to the president of the United States.

cavalry
A military unit on horseback.

colonel
A high rank in the military.

Congress
The collective term for the United States House of Representatives and Senate.

indecent
Not appropriate.

marshal
An officer who apprehends fugitives.

postmaster
A person who runs the post office.

primary
A vote held before an election to determine which candidates will run in that election.

unanimous
Complete agreement.

Wall Street
A street in New York City that is home to many financial institutions; used as a general term for finance in the United States.

For More Information

Books

Beckner, Chrisanne. *100 African-Americans Who Shaped American History*. Milwaukee, WI: World Almanac Library, 2015.

Calkhoven, Laurie. *Women Who Changed the World: 50 Amazing Americans*. New York: Scholastic Press, 2016.

Denenberg, Dennis. *50 American Heroes Every Kid Should Meet*. Minneapolis, MN: First Avenue Editions, 2006.

Visit 12StoryLibrary.com

Scan the code or use your school's login at **12StoryLibrary.com** for recent updates about this topic and a full digital version of this book. Enjoy free access to:

- Digital ebook
- Breaking news updates
- Live content feeds
- Videos, interactive maps, and graphics
- Additional web resources

Note to educators: Visit 12StoryLibrary.com/register to sign up for free premium website access. Enjoy live content plus a full digital version of every 12-Story Library book you own for every student at your school.

Index

About the Author

Todd Kortemeier is a writer from Minneapolis, Minnesota. He is a graduate of the University of Minnesota's School of Journalism & Mass Communication. He has authored many books for young people.

READ MORE FROM 12-STORY LIBRARY

Every 12-Story Library book is available in many formats. For more information, visit 12StoryLibrary.com.